IN A SUBMARINE EXPLORING THE PACIFIC

ALL YOU NEED TO KNOW ABOUT THE PACIFIC OCEAN

Children's Oceanography Books

BABY PROFESSOR

EDUCATION KIDS

Speedy Publishing LLC
40 E. Main St. #1156
Newark, DE 19711
www.speedypublishing.com
Copyright 2017

In this book, we're going to talk about the vast Pacific Ocean. So, let's get right to it!

Over 70% of our planet's surface is saltwater, which we call the ocean. The Earth has 5 oceans but you can actually think of them as one large body of water since they all flow into each other. The land where we live, the continents, separates the areas into 5 major oceans. The Pacific Ocean is the largest. The Atlantic Ocean is second largest, followed by the Indian Ocean, then the Arctic Ocean, and last the Southern Ocean.

WHERE IS THE PACIFIC OCEAN?

If you were traveling in a submarine and taking off from Asia or Australia, you would travel to the east across the vast Pacific Ocean to get to North or South America. The name of the ocean came from Ferdinand Magellan as he traveled around the world in 1521.

When he and his crew arrived there, the wind turned favorable for his ship. He named it "Mar Pacifico," which translates from Portuguese into "peaceful sea." The equator separates the ocean into north and south regions.

Nao Victoria (Ferdinand Magellan's Ship)

Clouds over the Pacific Ocean

HOW BIG IS THE PACIFIC OCEAN?

If you took all the surface of the land on Earth and pushed it all together, it still wouldn't be as big as the surface of the Pacific Ocean! That area is 30% of our planet's surface, about 169 million square kilometers or 65.4 million square miles. Even if you spent your whole life in a submarine, you couldn't visit every square mile of it.

HOW DEEP IS THE PACIFIC OCEAN?

··

The Pacific Ocean has deeper trenches than the other four oceans as well. The depth that's average is 12,467 feet deep. The deepest point in the ocean is located at the Mariana Trench. That point is called Challenger Deep after the Royal Navy ship, called the HMS Challenger, which first located it in 1875.

The scientists on board the ship used soundings as well as sent weighted lines down to measure the depth. There were no submarines or ways to explore that far down in the ocean at that time. Between the islands of Guam and Palau they recorded a depth that today we know is 10,994 meters or 36,070 feet. The Challenger Deep is the lowest point of the Earth's crust and was formed when two tectonic plates collided with each other.

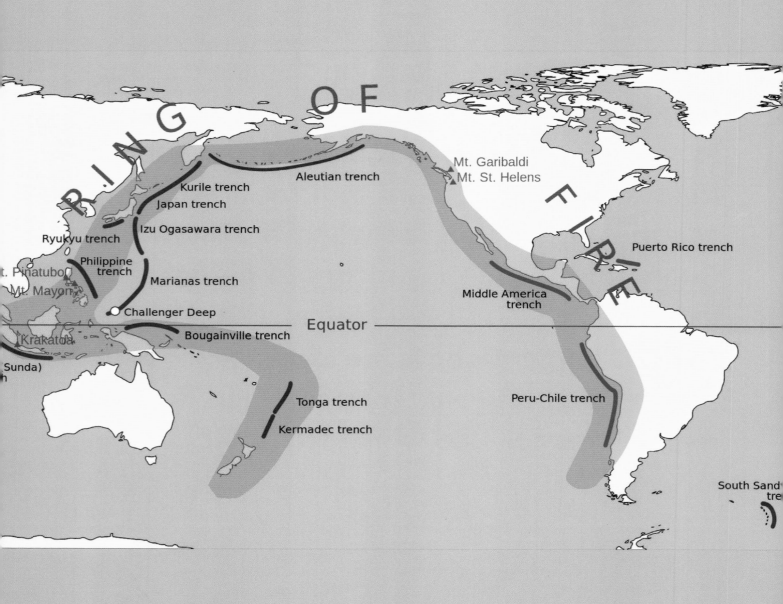

RING OF FIRE

Mt. Garibaldi
Mt. St. Helens

Aleutian trench

Kurile trench

Japan trench

Izu Ogasawara trench

Ryukyu trench

Philippine
trench

Marianas trench

t. Pinatubo
Mt. Mayon

Challenger Deep

Equator

Krakatoa

Bougainville trench

Sunda)

Tonga trench

Kermadec trench

Middle America
trench

Puerto Rico trench

Peru-Chile trench

South Sand
tre

WHAT IS THE RING OF FIRE?

About 75% of the world's volcanoes are actually under the Pacific Ocean and form a ring around its basin. This area has lots of earthquakes because of the volcanoes and movement of the tectonic plates. It affects the areas of land around it as well.

This is why the west coast of the United States, especially California, has so many earthquakes. Sometimes the force of the earthquakes causes tsunamis. These huge ocean waves caused by the seismic waves of the earthquakes cause massive destruction on land.

Mount Krakatoa

Mount Krakatoa in Indonesia is an island that is located on the ring of fire. In 1883 one of the biggest volcanic eruptions in recorded history happened there. The tsunamis that arose from that eruption were over 40 meters tall. The Krakatoa eruption was so powerful and the aftereffects so great that it impacted the global climate.

WHAT IS THE TEMPERATURE OF THE PACIFIC OCEAN?

The temperature of the ocean varies from 86 degrees Fahrenheit near the equator to freezing near the north and south poles. The lowest temperature recorded was 28 degrees Fahrenheit. If you were traveling in a submarine, the further you go down and away from sunlight, the colder it gets.

HOW MANY ISLANDS ARE IN THE PACIFIC?

There are more islands in the Pacific than any of the other oceans. Most of the islands are located in the South Pacific Ocean—there are over 25,000 of them! There are some countries that are largely made from groupings of islands as well.

Indonesia has over 17,000 and Japan has around 3,000. The second largest island in the world after Greenland is the country of New Guinea and it is located in the Pacific. There are six different types of islands:

Continental, these were part of a continent millions of years ago and then broke off

Barrier, these are separated from the shore by a sound or lagoon

Manam Volcano in Papua New Guinea

Mount Tavurvur in Papua New Guinea

Oceanic, these are also known as volcanic islands

Coral, these are formed by deposits of coral

Tidal, these are connected to the main land by land that is underwater at high tide

Artificial, these are formed by man

WHAT IS AN ARCHIPELAGO?

The Pacific Ocean is home to thousands of groups of beautiful islands. Clusters of islands form an archipelago. In addition to Indonesia and Japan, other countries that are formed from such clusters are New Zealand and the Philippines.

Palau Archipelago

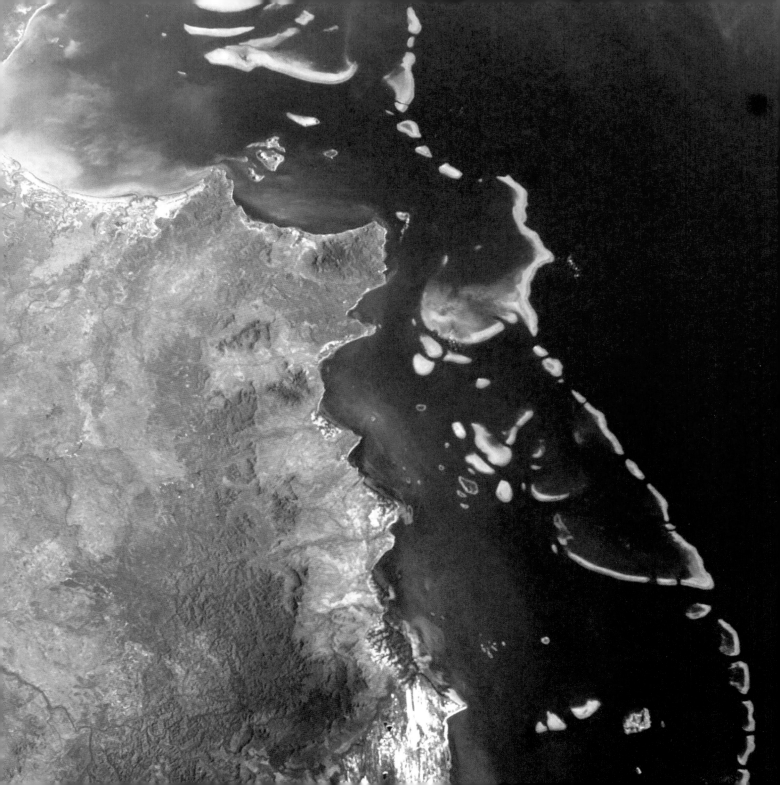

WHAT IS THE GREAT BARRIER REEF?

The largest reef system in the world is the Great Barrier Reef. It's located off the northeastern coast of the continent of Australia. It's the largest organic construction on Earth made of coral deposits that are over 1,400 miles long.

It's made of thousands of reefs and hundreds of islands. Six hundred types of coral are part of the reef and it's home to thousands of species of brightly colored fish, mollusks, and starfish. Sea turtles, dolphins, and sharks can be found there too.

GEOLOGICAL FEATURES OF THE PACIFIC OCEAN

Scientists believe that the Pacific Ocean formed after the breakup of the super-continent Pangaea. Two hundred fifty million years ago, the land on Earth was one super-continent. Eventually, the movement of the tectonic plates caused this supercontinent to break up and the oceans flowed around the pieces differently creating the oceans we know today.

THE OCEAN'S LIGHT ZONES

There are three light zones in the ocean. They are the sunlit, twilight, and midnight zones. They are also called the euphotic, disphotic, and aphotic zones. As we take our submarine down below the water, we travel in the top layer of the ocean.

This is the layer that gets the most amount of sunlight. It's called the euphotic zone. This level is from the surface to about 600 feet deep.

Just like on land, sunlight makes the process of photosynthesis work. On land, we have plants, bushes, and trees. In the ocean, we have tiny organisms called plankton.

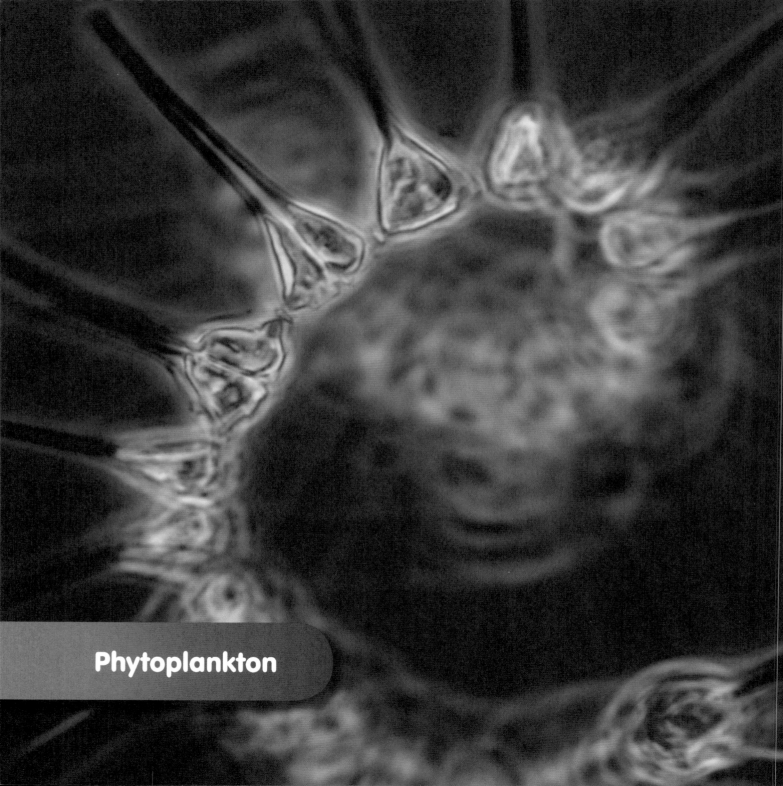

Phytoplankton

Plankton is the name of drifting organisms, both animals and plants, that live in this zone. There are three types of plankton:

Phytoplankton, these are algae that live on the surface and create their own food using photosynthesis just like land plants do

Zooplankton, these are tiny animals such as protozoa, small crustaceans, and jellyfish that feed on plankton, as well as eggs and larvae of other larger ocean creatures

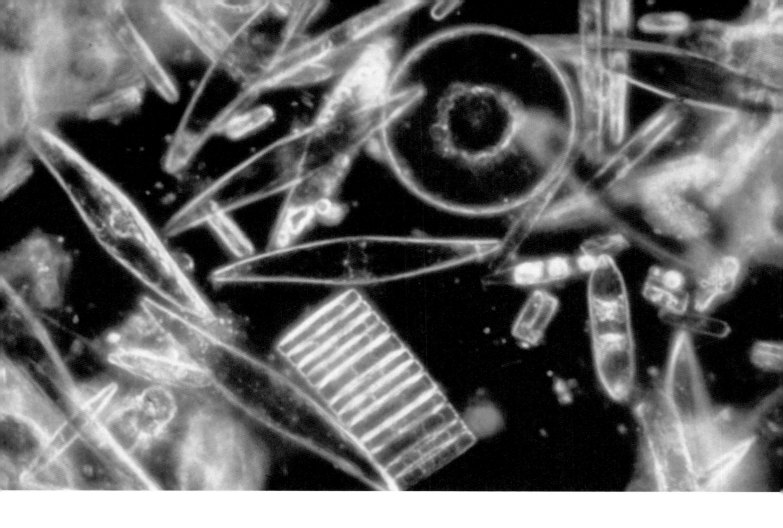

Bacterioplankton, **these are bacteria and archaea that absorb nutrients in the water**

Plankton are essential to ocean life because they provide the food for so many ocean creatures. About 90% of all ocean life lives in the top zone because there's so much food there.

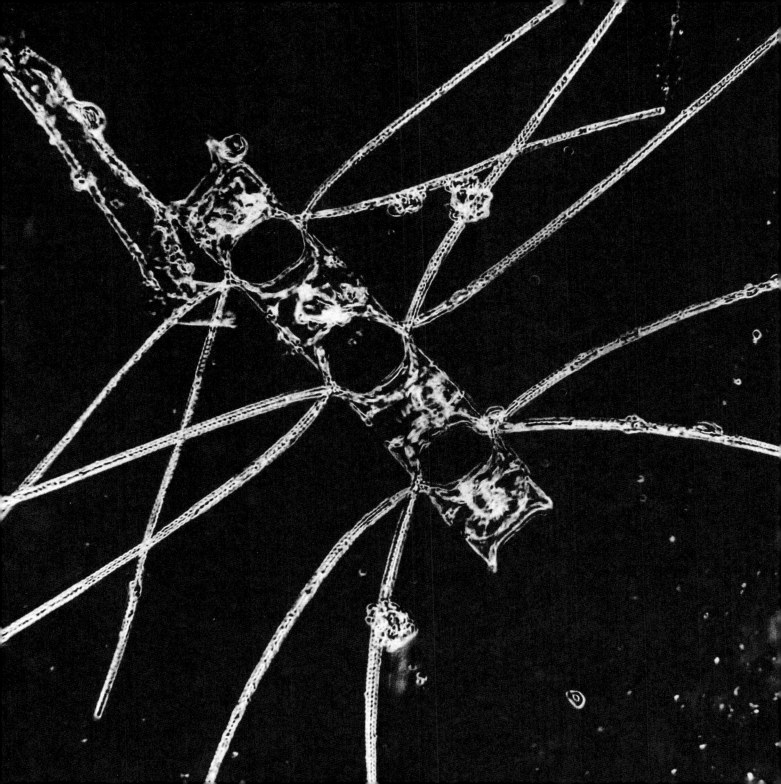

As we continue to go down, we reach the disphotic zone. This is the middle layer of the water. It begins at 600 feet down and goes to about 3,000 feet down, depending on how murky the water is. Plants can't live in this zone because there isn't enough sunlight for photosynthesis. The animals that live in this zone, especially in the lower depths, create their own light through chemical reactions.

Let's keep going down to the very bottom of the ocean. This is the aphotic zone. There's no light getting through down here. The pressure of the water is so high that the animals that live in this zone have adapted special physical characteristics allowing them to live here.

The few that survive in these depths feed off each other but also consume bacteria that thrive in the hydrothermal cracks at the very bottom of the deepest trenches. Marine biologists have recently found some new species at the bottom of the mariana trench. It was thought at one time that no form of life could survive the harsh pressure and intense cold at the very bottom.

TYPES OF ANIMALS AND PLANTS IN EACH ZONE

Each type of zone in the Pacific Ocean has different types of plants and animals.

EUPHOTIC PLANTS AND ANIMALS

In addition to the plankton, this zone has flowering plants such as eelgrass and mangroves that grow above water. Most type of fish, sharks and rays, jellyfish, sea turtles, coral, and seals are some examples of the types of animals you would find as we travel by in our submarine.

Many animals in this zone have counter-shading, which simply means that parts of their bodies are dark and parts of them are light colored to blend with the environment. Sharks are examples of animals with countershading.

Cuttlefish

DISPHOTIC ANIMALS

Most of the animals in this zone have large eyes and jaws. No plants exist here since there's not enough light. Cuttlefish, crabs, sea stars, and gray whales are a few examples of the types of animals we'd see here as we keep traveling.

APHOTIC ANIMALS

Animals that have adapted to live in this harsh, dark, cold environment are anglerfish, giant squid, tubeworms, and goblin sharks.

Tube worms

Awesome! Now you know more about the features of the Pacific Ocean and the creatures that live there. You can find more Oceanography books from Baby Professor by searching the website of your favorite book retailer.

Visit

BABY PROFESSOR
EDUCATION KIDS

www.BabyProfessorBooks.com

to download Free Baby Professor eBooks
and view our catalog of new and exciting
Children's Books

Printed in Poland
by Amazon Fulfillment
Poland Sp. z o.o., Wrocław